Fieldnotes on Ordinary Love

# Fieldnotes on Ordinary Love

KEITH S. WILSON

COPPER CANYON PRESS
PORT TOWNSEND, WASHINGTON

Cover art: Kellie Romany, *13, 24, 34, 35,* 2015. Oil on board, 8 × 10 inches.

Copper Canyon Press is in residence at Fort Worden State Park in Port Townsend, Washington, under the auspices of Centrum. Centrum is a gathering place for artists and creative thinkers from around the world, students of all ages and backgrounds, and audiences seeking extraordinary cultural enrichment.

LIBRARY OF CONGRESS CATALOGING-IN-PUBLICATION DATA

Names: Wilson, Keith S., author.
Title: Fieldnotes on ordinary love / Keith S. Wilson.
Description: Port Townsend, Washington : Copper Canyon Press, [2019] |
Includes bibliographical references.
Identifiers: LCCN 2018048848 | ISBN 9781556595615 (pbk. : alk. paper)
Classification: LCC PS3623.I585435 A6 2019 | DDC 811/.6—dc23
LC record available at https://lccn.loc.gov/2018048848

98765432 FIRST PRINTING

COPPER CANYON PRESS
Post Office Box 271
Port Townsend, Washington 98368

www.coppercanyonpress.org

To Mom and Dad, who never once, not even accidentally,
indicated anything but support. Who gave me more than
everything I have. To Bryan, my best friend, and to my
sister-in-law, Katelyn. To Faye, who cannot yet read,
but who has it in her blood.

# ACKNOWLEDGMENTS

*The Adroit Journal:* "I Investigate Terraforming in My Thirties," "6:45 p.m.," "Tercets," "A Unified Theory," "The Way I Hold My Hands"

*Because We Come from Everything* (Cave Canem online anthology): "Basilisk, as Seen in Reflection," "Mob"

*Best New Poets 2017:* "God Particle"

*Black Bone: 25 Years of the Affrilachian Poets:* "Mob"

*The Blueshift Journal:* "Fieldnotes"

*Crab Orchard Review:* "God Particle"

*Day One:* "I Find Myself Defending Pigeons"

*Drunken Boat:* "Basilisk, as Seen in Reflection," "The Gilead Transfer"

*Gulf Stream:* "String Theory," "The Test"

*Kindermeal:* "Basilisk, as Seen in Reflection," "Minotaur, Sixteen, Enters a Convenience Store," "Undine by the Drowned Cross"

*Kinfolks:* "Minotaur, Sixteen, Enters a Convenience Store"

Motionpoems: "Asterism"

*Narrative:* "Aubade to Collapsed Star," "Light as Imagined through a Body of Ice"

*Obsidian:* "Calf's Head and Ox Tongue"

*Passages North:* "A Short List of Grievances"

*pluck!:* "Cincinnati Windy Grays," "Driftwood"

*Poetry:* "Heliocentric," "Impression of a Rib"

*Split This Rock:* "Black Matters"

*Tidal Basin Review:* "The Lost Quatrain of the Ballad of a Red Field"

*Toe Good:* "Undine by the Drowned Cross"

*TriQuarterly:* "Augury," "Scrapbook"

*Vinyl:* "Yellow Journalism"

A very early draft of "A Short List of Grievances" (titled "Air") appears in *Undead: A Poetry Anthology of Ghosts, Ghouls, and More* (Apex Book Company).

"The Lost Quatrain of the Ballad of a Red Field" is after Gwendolyn Brooks's "The Last Quatrain of the Ballad of Emmett Till."

\*\*\*

To Nana, who had a library I still envy, a reading habit I can never match, and an intellect I aspire to reach.

To Aunt Shawn, who made time to read poetry to my brother and me, who performed it, and made it important.

To Regan, who changed everything.

To Diana, who taught me to listen and love.

To Jaquira Díaz, whose art and friendship astound me.

To Frank X Walker, who believed in me, and the Affrilachian Poets.

To Aricka Foreman, Meghan Dunn, Rio Cortez, Destiny Birdsong, Kenyatta Rogers, Angela Palm, Kateema Lee, Bianca Spriggs, Ladan Osman, and Katy Richey.

This book was made possible with fellowships and grants from Kenyon College, *Tin House,* Community of Writers, Miami Writers Institute, Ragdale, Vermont Studio Center, the MacDowell Colony, Ucross Foundation, the Poetry Incubator, Virginia Center for the Creative Arts, Poetry by the Sea, the Millay Colony for the Arts, Bread Loaf, Callaloo Creative Writing Workshop, *Arts & Letters,* Sundress Publications, the Baltic Writing Residency, *Adroit Journal, Narrative, Rhino Poetry,* Split This Rock, and Furious Flower Poetry Center.

To Cornelius Eady and Toi Derricotte and Cave Canem (and each of my groups!).

To the wait and social staffs at Bread Loaf.

To *Four Way Review* and *Obsidian.*

To Kima Jones and her team and the amazing work you do.

And to:

Margaret Rhee, Hafizah Geter, Jonterri Gadson, Rondal Robinson, Peter LaBerge, Francine J. Harris, Keith Leonard, Mitchell L. H. Douglas, Kris Yohe, Airea D. Matthews, Roger Reeves, Rachel Slotnick, Donna Spruijt-Metz, Ricardo Nazario y Colón, Randall Horton, Arthur Chapin, Tish Seabrook, Carly Joy Miller, Silvia Bonilla, Jessamine Chan, Allison Albino, Diana Delgado, Eve L. Ewing, Teneice Durrant, Crystal Good, Danni Quintos, Makalani Bandele, Ross White, Joy Priest, Brittney D. Cleark, Laura Swearingen-Steadwell, Quraysh Ali Lansana, Samuel T. Phillips, Tonya Wiley, Maya Marshall, Jayson P. Smith, Margaree Little, Mónica Jiménez, Amaris Selah, Michelle Peñaloza, Brian Simoneau, Dan Nowak, Kelly Norman Ellis, Ashaki M. Jackson, Nate Marshall, Jeremy Paden, Roberta Schultz, Iman Byfield, Parneshia Jones, Duriel E. Harris, Bernard Clay, Jude McPherson, Jericho Brown, Sami Schalk, Sally Wen Mao, Natasha Marin, Andrew Miller, Laura Goldstein, Cristina Correa, Ellen Hagan, Kyla Marshell, Christina Stoddard, Michelle Whittaker, April Gibson, Monét Cooper, L. Lamar Wilson, Amanda Johnston, and Jennifer Steele.

In memory of Nana, Papa, Uncle Steve, Uncle Mark, Rane Arroyo, Norman Jordan, and Danny Miller.

# CONTENTS

Fieldnotes on Ordinary Love

Aubade to Collapsed Star

You bankrupt the sun, underwater
statue. Dark galaxy of faults, our bed

a garden of the littlest sighs
of our waking. Our room, abstract.

Our body heat in space, the condensation
as the light makes heaven of it. We're early,

curved and signatory, the sheets
paler than the sky and made

immaterial. My hands confused
for want of your hands

or waist. Rolling, what claims
we make of earth, what is inferred and isn't

sure, what the undersides of the leaves
of the forest floor are called. Your breath.

My limbs and yours. All of space
cannot be space. Arousing

patches in the grass. A mouse,
I never said to you. Invasion of clover, black

pollen of your hair. Only yesterday
I said I love. The opposite of stars.

The moon's clear effects
on the sea. In sleep, no body

is the lead. I am dreaming imaginary
numbers of fruit flies, mercury and birdsong,

and the trash collector, and the water glittering
beige in the street. Of the Milky Way as portrayed

by the swirl of your waves. I ought to have married you
against the ifs of this world, out of flux

with all the dishes and the dust
on the books, and your late

mornings, each movement
I have missed like this, and I, accustomed

to the wall when I awake,
the exodus of your laugh, mascara.

## Tercets

love it's only gotten worse my father can't stop
saying your name like a war his nation lost or a miracle

that saved him from an undertow unprompted
you rise like a body from a lake before dinner

grace has never been more biblical than in the gasp
about your name the quiet

being the inverse of a heartbeat i depended on a season
for which there is no dress and i say yeah

and i say yeah dad but you love are a tragedy
in my father's eyes my reflection having just shaved

my skin is tender i say before he can say
i remember yes she was just like that i cannot change

that i remember my love i swallow
my hands every day taking the place of your hands on the table

## The Way I Hold My Hands

I can't imagine my father wishing he would rather be
anything. Once upon a time, he was a watermelon
growing from a box. His mother died. His father beat
the blush out of him, and teardrops dripped black
from his face into his food. My father's father made him eat
his dinner through himself, the Miracle Whip salad spangled
like the garden in dew. This isn't a figure of speech: my father ate
his blood. It's hard to think he must have been young. He made me stop
all my life. He told me not to be a girl. Whatever I was doing,
of course I stopped. He kissed me on the top of the head
before I went to bed each night. He was always there. He read
to my brother, he read to me from a book of animals. This is a fox's paw.
This is a bear's. He told me, I'll give you something
to cry about. He never touched me. Bear claw, I said. Winters are easier
for bears. I spread my fingers over his. No, my father said.

## Impression of a Rib

*Le Café-concert aux Ambassadeurs* (1876—77), Edgar Degas

i have a red dress and no eyes.
i have a dress that is blood-
red and i have eyes that don't blink

when the balcony sucks in. my dress is a beet
swollen with thought, and hangs like a body
on my body. i have eyes that don't blink

at being seen. i was halfway finished
before i saw i'd begun. my dress drips
down the center. my eyes are needle holes

and my dress is an over-red thread. i hang
my words in the air by their feet, limp
and damp, and my dress is my only laugh

that is actually red. my eyes
are the backs of moons, and afterward men
jest us like children, and smoke,

and women who have been my dress
circle their stomachs with their hands.
i'm an actress. this is not my mother

tongue. i have a dress that is
yellow. my lines are written by a parisian
man. we met in london. i came dancing

out like god upon a crimson wave. my dress hung
like a question or a suddenness. he wrote me
coming out this way, he says, to make me

7

like a lioness. the constellations are full
of dead women, he says. he says
my dress is the coat of a great lion.

i turn like the blood inside
a rose. the crowd is a great gasp. i can feel myself
become a pear. it's as if you haven't taken

pills, he says. i still have that dress.
it's not too blond or red. you can grasp
it with your eyes, he said, the way you wear it.

6:45 p.m.


And the door opened in, as a sapphire
asserts a certainty of blue and you, through the hall

like an alarm, and my body determined some parcel
of space, your lips in passing,

and you reclined into the silence of the bed,
and must always have found yourself there while I was not

thinking. How surely you dreamed. And what was in your head
was a better thing than art, or rather, it was more beautiful

to wonder than to know; the absent-minded stretches
of you where I might, while sitting, hit a deer. What made you finally

stand? It's astounding I never upset you
of your mystery. *Loving* is a misnomer, because you are expected

of your heart's opinion on a sentence that is never completed,
even as you're having it. Nothing must be more free than the feeling

of the right to leave. You were really something
like a cutting the way you laid yourself in water

every night reading. But the days average on and the planets
circle round us like sharks. God, it's pretty.

But what does any of it mean?

## A Unified Theory

Call it aesthetics or beauty, but you privilege
a portion of her face—let's say your eyes
are accustomed to a certain side—

the way you have a specific space to lay
your body when sleeping with her first in your bed
and then in any other, any horizontal plane.

Some would say this isn't real symmetry,
but you know of course it is,

with you as the vertical, the folding line,
and through no intention on either side,
her face is curiously balanced

(yours in hers for all you know); imagine
a card tower as custom-built for the hold of the moon—your chest,

the satellite holding. A million instances in which you've drawn

a complicated cursive R. Every time, stop to think, starting
in the same place, say, her right eye to the curve of the bridge of her nose,
her cheekbones, and you find yourself
like a contractor building over and over the same home.

She takes her steps too, though you never think to ask
whether she begins first with the plates or the spoons,

and when you tell her, you mean it
as a working definition. Or specifically, this is why

she cannot help but be, to you. And that is only her face—
you have awakened by the mouth

of this wave, and again this wave, again,

for so long as to let the name change. What arced her
like the inside of a pitcher of water

and makes you a cartographer you cannot know by this,
but here you are, facing

this little world with the only science
you know. So what that it's easy to love
a country when your body has grown into its shell?
So what if you play favorites with this history?

You think, what if I am stuck like this? What if

I never change? So what.
Never change.

Moments are not for revision—
if they are lived honestly, they are open to one interpretation
only. They make you like a child.

Of course that's what they make.

The Test

All ways are better ways of talking more honestly of love
than the act itself, which, yes, is love I guess,

but then is always also something else,
since I am thinking of your scare (we

think), and whatever love is, it isn't this obsessive
worry. Or actually, love is

fret, since that's the music-making
bump of a guitar. You know by now we are callus

and cacophony, our minds
and bodies are at once

belief, and sublime,
subliminal, and liminal

too, and you laugh, which shatters a glass
in me (I wanted you

to laugh), and I managed the silence, I know, I know,
I am hardly making sense, but I am trying

actually to break a certain ice: notice the light playing games

with the wall beside my bed the night I realize I cannot have you
leave, and while I am ever a series of periods,

you are not. A pyramid

between us, a great wonder
that says a little something about permanence

to us now, and how, when we might finally have it, we shed
our skins and flee. The problem is in saying forever

at exactly the same time. On three:
this is us trying. You called it karma, you said

this is what we get for cheating. But consider what we have;
everything the world is not might also be a blessing.

Fieldnotes

1

in physics dark matter isn't made
of anything. it's a free citizen

that passes
unburdened through the field, through itself,

through you—

2

it helps to observe from a distance:
the field, for instance,

as a statement

the south has chosen to make,
the way whiteness too
is often rhetorical, as when an older student remarks

in those beginning days that only he observed mlk's holiday
while his black friends, working, did not

3

sometimes love is a black dot
in a field

sometimes, suddenly
it is not

4

or how can black be

the absence
of all color? take this cruiser. see the light strike blue off the car like copper
          through a fountain

5

there is a difference between what is fair and what is just,
for instance,

it is fair
that i try
to love your skin even when it is not touching my own

6

whiteness is an alibi, the way the officer was like a steam-
engine
          only i could see

7

inside where nothing shows i am of course not black
but that does not matter

to the field

8

some colors are indistinguishable
at night. *put your hands behind your back*

a different cop once asked me.
it was so sincere. he was so

polite

9

as a boy you learn to know the inside
without being required to feel it

as when, now, i understand a bucket
            or a hood

10

he asks my girlfriend not if she is white
since even in this light

what we are is obvious

but instead he speaks philosophically:

*ma'am* he asks
*are you here of your own free will*

11

sometimes whiteness is a form itself
of hyperbole. try this:

sit in a field. then try reading

andrew jackson's quotes on liberty
only
pretend they are being written by his slaves

12

look at the word black
on the paper
& you will see a definite black,      a kind,

a certainty,

or if you see nothing at all that of course
is a kind of black too

13

by the road
my father showed me cotton
once

*look at that*
he said

Asterism

It's funny to think now of that silence, with you
at the desk reading, and me writing on the couch,

separately, and the meaning of that nothing
happening all around us still

were you available now to hold
my hand, or if you continued to sit sometimes

in this chair, tired of the world outside
of us, or if I anymore wrote

about possibilities other than this, or the curve of your
nose, the bridge beneath my lips—

that is,
if the silence of the two of us

were predicated by my being able now to reach you,
how that quiet, that night, in this room, might seem a comfort,

but instead of that, the candles
between, and neither of us with anything

in particular to say, the quiet trembles,
because your voice isn't a feather I can hold

but a thought I draw
across my throat when I close my eyes—

I am trying to say that though the mass of the absence
has already gone, a world

revolves around it still, the two of us
who try to speak like stars that cannot be heard

because of all the things they say of space.

## The Lost Quatrain of the Ballad of a Red Field

AFTER A MURDER,

IN A QUIET SUBURB

Some man's lovely mother, a fence, picks at
      her jewelry in the light.
She sits quiet, clean, in a room,
        drinking a cooled white wine.
She thumbs a jersey,
      not sorry, sublime,
still bound by her stomach to her boy,
      to the long red lines
           her son made dragging a man,
                  screaming, through a field.

# The Floor Scrapers

*Les raboteurs de parquet* (1875), Gustave Caillebotte

whatever they say of the heart, the truth is this:
we embody our hands. every morning i have my look at them.
my hands cupping my face, a bowl of water.
what will i make of these pliers, this filigree

of clams? i love how the light lollops from knuckle
to knuckle like a fox across a lake.
what is the rest of me but a daydream
of angles? what but a happening of curves?
when i am freest, when i'm at peace, it is only the light

making palatable my hands, in a grasp,
in a reach like this, as when a man offers his

in extension and becomes, before me,
a basilica, and i watch the gleam of the fish-throated
muscles of the back, the narrow bones
and knees and, i say again, the knuckles,
each a chamber for a whole religion

performed by the hands—hands
doing, possessing and pressing firmly
to the ground to scrape—if you've ever taken the dark
meat from a thigh bone by your teeth?—like that—
and his back is a crowbar for the actions
being completed by the palms of him,

his intersections (the fingers lolling over each other like men
on a rocking train) and i see the light and the labor both

and the ordinary somersaults of the rib cage
and viscera (they say the heart), but i see the fingers
motioning like this too, and my own hand, curled

like a conversation made after light has ceased
to bluster in the caverns of the eye
and sits thick and pleasant as a man having
worked himself religious—again, they say the heart.

# Scrapbook

*after Ladan Osman*

i. look—in the middle distance the siren screams
like a fatherless boy,

unashamed. ii. sisyphus hikes up her dress.
she labors pushing,

always a man,

and if she shrugs, he rolls atop her
or the town at the foot of the hill. or a man, calling himself sisyphus, knocks
and says push is a man's verb

but she can help. or else,

he says, quiet. iii. it's said we are afraid
of what we don't understand. who

among us is shaken by latin? we are terrified of what might
overtake us. sadness, marriage, spanish,

rain. iv. like a sextant he angled himself as if
(as if!) to kiss. his hands in the ocean of her
eyes and his knee pressed against the air

like a rudder. v. how can i make you
understand? as a boy i held a bell in my hand. and i grew

to be a man who looks back

on that bell. vi. what is there
to say? that was yesterday. vii. the first thing odysseus decides
when he returns is to cock his bow. fire

in the crowd. over and again, bullets move
at flirtatious angles. viii. in the city, the first november rain

laps at a set of heels. ix. a family of plantains.
no one speaks

their name. actually,

a silence, even when they are perfect and brown.
every domestic, familiar,

unpretty thing. x. i'll say it again:

if a hand is big enough it doesn't matter
what you call it. xi. the story of orpheus and the bear is this—
orpheus, of course,

sings. his wife is distinguished
by her marriedness

to orpheus. jumping ahead: he left behind his clothing, his furniture
and everything. xii. there is an old story

of a man. that is the story.

there is an old story of a woman
that the old story of the man spoke over.
i am his son. xiii. imagine here the voice

of a woman. xiv. a list of all that is fixed:
only the ground.

## Pigeonheart

let us embody the now-extinct passenger pigeon
squab each other       cede

let us the oven door of evening
like extinction

be bound to hunger
hunted and haze like sudden summer

we ought glaze like water

curry
want

           love

                    be

           infinity's honey

glory but bitter and crisp
kale and plume
                    and ungainly thirst

i want to learn butter
lord

i had better    let's

pickle tart and faith for each other
as through a sieve
as if there's nowhere else but we

seeming vs. meaning vs.
the grease that glees the metal

heaven yeast my water
            outfacing

what taste is surely taste
what thought is

                    actually

under question

love swells hypothesis
love fools

        under it

the body will again and again
reduce i think to jelly

A Short List of Grievances

First, you are invisible,
which is another word for Jesus

she's gone. Second, the medulla oblongata makes you
automatic, so even when I am not thinking
of your hips, I am

thinking of your hips (the dreams I have dreamed
of being loosed like a sparrow would pronounce themselves

into wilder dreams if I were a bird already.
I would have to eat nothing until I was thin as the air

and I'd baffle the moon, my simple machines turning
the mobile of the sky. I could be

ready. Heave and release.
Only the nothing of a bird).

Third,
You are right. I am cabinetry.
I'm a man that needs to know conclusively

that he is empty. Your name,
you know, is a midnight call. I am talking too much

about air and hardly about breath—
who do you think, really,

makes me lift my chest? This should be simple.
But it never is. Consider the wing,

to which the burden of air
becomes the burden of flight.

## Ode to the Glow

glad iodine of my heart / haunt /

lo / rarefied metal /

o mercury / i cannot touch /

your edges / bare /

pulse and hex and sirenize /

our breakneck happening / passion /

the dates / the hurried current /

in between / late /

uranium /

a half-life without you / in my dreams /

how i had you / caramelized black /

mold / at heart /

i hold / i know / i have /

my lowest hum /

cyanide / my zeal / ethereal /

a kingdom for sleep / anything alas /

to never see you / atlantis /

the impossibility / my love / the statue /

the broken armed beauty / the care /

exactitude /

i made you / stay /

terminal and fleet / fantasy /

hang with me / babylon /

in the garden /

my will / or will you /

manifest /

be / breathe / canary / zyklon b /

glow or flower / bear this with me / curie /

read hematopoietic / hearts /

and sirens / glass / cartography /

cure me / of my breath /

to catch / hell /

to pray / to come / to fawn / to sea /

## Calf's Head and Ox Tongue

> ca. 1882, Gustave Caillebotte, 29 × 21 in.,
> the Art Institute of Chicago

Here stands Minotaur, before the painting,
   rigid, shaven, his Nikes (amazing—
how can he afford Nikes?) pewter blue, impossibly clean, seen
   clearly here in the track light.
His far-apart eyes, deep as Sabalan's crater,
one earbud in the tepee of his left
ear, the other tucked like a secret in his pocket. Minotaur in name and race

and inclination, here as witness

to the young tongue's fashionable sag.
Oil on canvas. Three and one-half pounds
of meat. And dangling, and keeping pace with the tongue,
a pitted head. What once was calf, painted.
What once was the truth of a tongue.
   A window, and a set of displaced
bricks. "This is the power

that a master has over us, the grace—" says the teacher, raising
his voice. *Like a god. A fucking swan,* Minotaur thinks. Right.

      Far away, his classmates laugh.
The gallery, on this side, is suddenly empty as the stomach

of a bell. Dead as his cell phone. Only Minotaur remains;
   everyone else is looking through a different frame
on the other side of the wall, at a painting with proud men
   and guarded women too, above reflection,

under umbrellas. But here, at the head and tongue,
Minotaur stands close enough to smell

the sage breath of the calf, or the must
of the canvas at least. The song in his ear, Rage
Against the Machine. No harmony at all
flows down into his backward knees,
                    and he doesn't see
representation
(he learned that word, *representation,* about objects
only),

          but instead imagines love
of paint. Abandon.

Minotaur was that, once. Left

like this, at a petting zoo: his horns
not yet formed and his prayers still determined
to keep them sheathed deep within his cratered head.
          How he starved to be right
and human as all the other children romped
through the dirt, flaunting their long and golden hair,
absently feeding the swans. But Minotaur paid
                    his twenty-five cents and threw his seed

into the bushes. He had hoped to grow a tree.
Even now—here, in this museum—but back then as well,
          Minotaur's recurring dream

has been of being a gazelle: his legs slender with athletic gears
that apotheosize him through the air

like a bullet. Of course he relates to herd animals. Here

in the gallery there is no room to run.
*Everyone here watches golf,* he thinks,
and Minotaur stays well behaved as Tiger
Woods as he eyes the calf's head, white as pine, the ox tongue, a rose,

in silence. He cannot see whatever makes it universal
                    from around the hook
in his cousin's nose. Everywhere around, the faces seeming
to understand. Maybe this painting is in his language too,

and he must only try to read the book.
Or not to read, but translate the waxen

head, glowing dead, into a vowel, the musculature of tongue
into, maybe, a generic letter
aitch, or look into the tender
where the horn almost touches the medium
rare, as if he did not see the intimacy
there. His mother tongue is hidden in a larger tongue
he cannot step far enough back to see. Or his father's

tongue, hanging there, circumcised.
Being this objective hurts;
mastery is a brand glowing white. Nikes

squeak as Minotaur leans back nervously.
Paint flecks coagulate into an order. He paces,
and his movement smooths the colors into lines.
        His heart becomes a wide-eyed animal.
He can think of nothing but the feeling of being surrounded by a race.
He has to run.
        Minotaur begins a jog

but is scolded by a man in ironed
slacks, walks rapidly instead—the calf's head

and ox tongue coming with him, rolled like an *R* in his pocket,
his daughter or his son. His father, or his father's hands

never able to paint. Minotaur cannot see past the gallery,
feels fenced in by white picket faces. To his right,
the artist as a brightness over women at the park. Farther, artist as hard
marble, in the nude, killing

lion. Minotaur feels like a deer shot with light, turns suddenly to artist
as steam enraptured by the cobalt under glass, crosses
artist as girls retrieving fruit after dance. He can see water
lilies being kept alive on this wall, the hay

where his father lay across many paintings. Several shades
of different sun. Minotaur

sees through the glass, and the glass itself,
and the reflection of the glass. Artist as gluten-free

bread, artist as jam,
as sandwich, and, turned around, a portrait of the poor.
Artist as dramatic, forceful choice,
as a million points of light,
two million points of dark impressions. Like all the true religions lost
in God's married name. Just a moment, Minotaur thinks.

Still life with whomever.
          Crazy
layers. Still life just before the flies.

## God Particle

You were the smallest thing. Think
of the terrified play

of rabbits in the grass before the street:
fractional, they are

ants reverse engineering the desperate flapping
of the land. Even less.

They are mindless
atoms unaware of themselves or the heart

between matter and time. You were smaller and more
precious than that. If you imagine

them littler than eyelashes—the tissue-paper carapace,
thorax—all of it—the bones of ships

under glass—if you can imagine the elements of those atoms, of those ants
and rabbits, as not the skin of the observable universe

but the whisper upon which we built a hearth,
you'll understand. Call it want,

or dependence, or sleep. Call it eventide or
home; how to summarize a galaxy

          with a night
—we are impossible

to fix. Dust motes and a million paths of light.
I know.

Eventually it all comes down to an
        admission.

Whatever my failings—didn't I come to it,

        eventually?

# Mob

*and they were coming toward him in rough ranks.*
*In seas. In windsweep. They were black and loud.*

Gwendolyn Brooks, "Riot"

All day was filled with the floating dead
of clouds. Children

throwing birds, guns for thumbs
and forefingers.

My heart is a mine shaft of canaries
and shells.

My smell is filled with flying
and what a sky this is.

The northern European still lifes
depicted so many flowers.

Lying on my side, looking. Where his eyes might be.
The dead teach us that kind of patience.

How different the drawings of a people must be
who have always had this kind of time.

&ast;&ast;&ast;

A brief history of rope:
some of us are brown
as starvation.

Happenstance is the color
of our eyes.

\*\*\*

What happens when you stare into the sun?
A crow is born. From here, I think
about the image of God.

He set jagged stars
in the square holes of us.

\*\*\*

And what are groups of us called?
It is an unkindness

of ravens, for instance. For instance,
        a dole (an offering)

of doves. We've always been more glorious as a flock.
Groups of us are congregations.
What is more godlike than peace (other than insurgence),

than quiet, as of the breathing of evening
birds, the low warble of our people in the trees.

\*\*\*

Sometimes a dream is a fist you grow into,
but more often, a routine, like watering a weed in your stomach.

\*\*\*

We haven't been made afraid of trees. Nor the bottoms of cars.
Windows, the gavel, the sea.

\*\*\*

A feather is caught in the rapture of a fence,

keeps struggling—can't come to terms—
cannot unthink that it's a bird.

                    * * *


What gives the ground the right
to gravity? No building.

I want to widen the eyes of God.
Every amendment has followed through
against our bodies.

Icarus leapt. We will fly,
be black together in the sun.

## Cincinnati Windy Grays

i only asked for a pop.
i have never got to see a bird stay still.
yesterday i heard a man say a word
that ran my heart
away. i can't wait
to be hard. heard. even to be grit.
my teeth. my fingernails chalked, sidewalks
and the roots of trees
coming through the wood ceiling
for me. one day
you'll let me put a butterfly in your ear.
i'll have things. when i'm older. if
the streetlights are on, jump curbs, try flying.
up and up. living
things move. the way watermelon is soft
in your mouth, i am almost a cloud.
there are flies. here.
there are small things moving, still.
before that,
there were high lights and good
and plenty, flowers.
i dreamed of you. it was loud and bright
and moving. fast. it was moving too fast.
i was lying in the grass.
breathing.

Minotaur, Sixteeen, Enters a Convenience Store

This is Minotaur—his name, his race—
brazenly alone. Left,

       right, left, right, left—he walks. Nothing amazing.
       Nothing worth reporting. Again he finds himself shadowed

       by a clerk. Now, in the far corner
       of the store (or is he being too sensitive?),

       he swells suddenly with hunger, holsters
       the heft of his phone. His pockets bulge

       under the breath of the worker, bearded, who stocks
       beside him. Minotaur knows a man is always ready to take

          the good dare of a life.
          As simple as a pop,

          as effortless to pilfer as a carton of milk or OJ.
          A man's blood courses like this and wants. His fingers prick.

          More than anything, Minotaur wants to feel his fingers
          tingle.

          The moment a child disappears
          is never caught on camera. Only black and white—only another,

          another evening, artful even, punctuated just
          by the silent hammer of a man's fearful eyes.

               *Look here, boy.* Minotaur can pull
               the hammer back.

*Look here.*
This is his hot

breath, giving soul
to the cooler's glass. O Asterion, try

to live. Here, *boy,* is his heavy lead.
Here is the gap in the hood

of a savage jacket.
Even the jacket wants to live.

Maybe man
is deadlier in fractions.

Minotaur carries the 9, makes himself
full.

## Undine by the Drowned Cross

I see that Bibles never last;
they shift to skin.
Words bloat
      when filled with sea.
Time and nature part them.
      I know Christmas
by the slow float of Judith's paper snow.
By disintegration. I try
to catch meaning in my mouth,
          pray
the seeds grow in me like yeast.
Rise. Please.
I cannot read your Word, I've only in passing
      heard of
salvation. It is an addiction new to me.
Don't give me that. Instead, I beg:
      please. Please.
Let my soul be.

## Driftwood

The driftwood's brown
eyes are blue
as the white lap of the lake
and the face and hands
are ellipses, sober
and round. What time is it—
the sun's still stuck
spinning the sky all purple and white
(I have, you know, a waiting
wife), but wow, how the wind swings
him good—boy, fetch
us the keys—and the fishing here's good too,
whether from a shore
or a tree. Reel
him in good, right there, before he
splits. He must be
smarter now with water
where his thoughts ought
to be. Go tell the rest—you say you know his son—
       I said what time
is it—and what about his tongue?
I say our boys never lie: some fish
caught the roundness of his eye.
What about his tongue now?
What a sight he used to be.
That chest full of drawers,
those shoulders full of squirrels,
that boat stacked in
with worms. What a jamboree,
but such a waste;
my shoes are dirty
and that boy

could shine the black
off almost anything.
I'm only repeating an old Confederate joke—
boy, I'm saying it again, what time is it right now?

# I Investigate Terraforming in My Thirties

Soon enough I find an Earth-like
planet, but how Earth-like is only like, is like

how a kiss may be alike
but isn't quite,

or how every photo from Kentucky—
how you used to sigh—is only

now a likeness. Or how this bandaged light
upends the bruise that became

the sky: I liked you, I like liked
you. And we held each other

as we made our child-
hoods hush; we strained

to merge like trees into a custom. We held
to each other's hands

even when our notes
were misaligned. We would,

without half-trying, alight one upon the other.
What is gravity to our horns? We reached

and tore each other plain as walls
or erstwhile countries,

and the dream became a sun—
beneath me, the land, the fade

of wing, my every instrument
a lyre's vital music, my every simile, a flame.

Augury

I'm close to certain with my choice of pigeon—this one—
under the bridge as I return from the Walgreens

where I bought the pill. Its head bulges
with a legacy of green and white

feathers; magnanimous wings that decide not
to fly, its mind all right with crumbs, the hope of men

doing right, rather than whatever men take it upon themselves to do—
whatever they want, walk at night—the skyscrapers

long along the distance. What to do
or what there is to do or whether doing

is good—I remember being told I should never touch
a baby bird in its nest. That afterward,

the mother would rather let her children starve.
It isn't true. But how many eggs

has the fantasy kept safe,
how many feathers made elegant, my hands clean and far away

to fold snowflakes or cranes? Whatever I like.
Card towers. Circles of light

across the street. You ought to be able to see through it all.
I wonder what is the sound of this silence

without my silence. My pigeon flies
to a place I can't follow. I have no idea what to do.

I love how you never find their bodies, how they never rest their eyes. I love how their breasts are comforters unfolding by their breath. I love that pigeons live in the city, that underestimation never stopped a pigeon from unlatching itself or being old. I want them all unspooling in the air, and bridges that are half sigh and half pigeon. I want to harbor their coo and utilize it for energy. I want to learn to use them the way they want to be used. I want to pigeontail into a quiet night, to let their oddness sit in our hands. You can never know a language until you quiet your own. I want people to write about them. Their leaving ships for land, or standing on their own on a marble statue in the shimmer of a field. I want to talk about the term *rock dove,* argue over whether or not it's imperialist. I want the media to implicate us in the pigeon problem, for a couple to sit with their asparagus and kids and realize none of this is far from them, whatever we think. I want oils and watercolors and inks. I want still life with pigeons, since not a one has ever been portrayed with soul: a flight of them around old bread. And how they're all the same. How all the world is here with them in hate, since they are rats adorned with angel wings, and the children down the street are free to chase their drag; they want to see a pigeon's rouge entirely. Let the pigeon have her pigment. Consider the pigeon's brown and green and everything, the brandishing of his nakedness to the sun, as if nothing is absolute. I love the pigeons' shoulders, tongues, and wedding nights. I love the pigeon's place in history, their obsession with living in the letters of our signs. I love their minds, or what I've come to believe is their theology. Who knows? Let the pigeons speak. Ask the closest pigeon for his number, for her middle name, if they are ready to die, if the sky gets crowded enough to consider war, if their stores are closed on Sundays. I want to be ready for them to be just like us, but more ready for them to be completely different. I don't want to waste any time tracing a pigeon's god to Abraham. I want to get started. Some of us feed pigeons. I love, sometimes, our care. I love, I think, the park bench. I love apples, but I do not love pears. The weather. I love the pigeons, the revolution of wheel to sky. I love the newspaper graying in a different air.

## Yellow Journalism

another limping complicated animal,
the sky.

this hog house called a home.
the tour guide chirping.

this plantation will live forever
like a liar

or a cricket from under the stairs.
i am an alien. my father is at home.

visitors are welcome
to come in period-appropriate dress, she says.

dad, take off your shirt.
i'll go fetch the chains.

       ***


from littleness, i told stories.
a litany saved me

from pouring blacktop in kentucky
like my father.

slipping like a feather
in it. i'd be less

a dreamer, dad. think of how close
we'd have become.

       ***

a good joke begins with a lie.
catching myself naked like a runaway

in the mirror, i see, i repossess
the bird of my father's body.

his place, lessened.
more open, more light.

just before the beasts
knew that they would drown, bare laughter

from the dove's wings.
is this the dream my mother saw?

# The Gilead Transfer

*Arriving* _____ *Sixteenth Street*

Signs come and go,
meaningless. The spectrum
of his dreams bleeds like gasoline
on water. Basilisk witnesses proofs and other
axioms—possibility that stirs
in the dead eyes of a building,
pockmarked glass,
lynched blinds,
the cicada-husk of an air conditioner

left trigger-cold. He's hung up on the inch of wood he sees
that demarcates bus-stop benches. Bench-
dividers that keep men
from sleep. And patched women, children screaming

                              one another's names explosive

against the chill. In that car wash lies
the gray sacrifice of the lottery—tickets
purchased from a man who still wears hats, who sells, as well,
rolling papers, bowls, and razor blades.
The not-unhappy people who greet and brag, as if they know
one another.

     \* \* \*

Even the graffiti behind the graffiti fades
to white—what a tragedy the sun must make
of the children. The bus sags
about him like denim. Basilisk is taken
on a new line to an old street.

Migration is the mother of cities, he tells himself.
      His people!
The yellow whale is full—
its wheels spin a black prayer
from the street.

Basilisk's Broken Window Theory:
Empty buildings cannot keep their windows.
These apartments catch rocks
in the proud gaps of their teeth, cave
into themselves like tired mothers.
It would be cheaper to keep
them occupied.

         \* \* \*

When hope is the shock wave that hits a bus, it is butterfly wings.

At the other end of the transfer, north of here, where the city opens up, another
place. The basilisk in tourist clothes. Dogs pulled back, politely.
Neon joggers veer. Businesses take the bars from their windows; neighbors
plant them like peonies in their lawns. Children play more
like children. Passing the basilisk, a woman constricts her body and her coat.

(In that moment, a loud crack
      like frozen pipes beneath—dark thunder breaks below the steps!)

        This is not the north
side. He is transferred. But what is that sound,
and that pale white light?

*Sometimes I feel discouraged*—Remember being southern?
*And think my work's in vain*—Out the window, all the little girls.
*But then*—The bus billows with a broke

mass of bodies—*the Holy Spirit*—All change is tender.
               Warmth beats
against the basilisk, up-rises him—
        all the little girls—*Revives my hope again!*—
humming up the benumbed blood from under the church of him.

        Sing low: *Strawberry shortcake, huckleberry pie*—
His eyes close. Maybe this is another dream?
Some kind of drum is beating. Breath runs out—There is a balm!—
a song goes slowly in

        *There is a balm!*             *There is a balm!*—

## Black Matters

after D.H. Lawrence

shall i tell you, then, that we exist?
there came a light, blue and white careening,
the police like wailing angels
to bitter me.

and so this:
dark matter is hypothetical. know
that it cannot be seen

in the gunpowder of a flower,
in a worm that raisins on the concrete,
in a man that wills himself not to speak.

gags, oh gags.
for a shadow cannot breathe.
it deprives them of nothing. pride

is born in the black and dies in it.
i hear our shadow, low treble
of the clasping of our hands.

dark matter is invisible.
we infer it: how light bends around a black body,
and still you do not see black halos, even here,

my having told you plainly where they are.

Basilisk, as Seen in Reflection

Entering back into the bus she catches him
in her gaze. She roams him openly—he hides
his eyes. The woman cannot slay

her urge to overcome this living painting,
unwrap the strange of him like eyelids
from an onion. She asks about his skin
(does it burn?), and she writes her number, makes an offer.

He looks down at himself. Under her gaze he feels drawn
tight. In the reflection he can see his cubism,
the misaligned hell of his shirt. He struggles
too much, wars with his fingers (stiff

beneath the killing look). She reaches out and touches
him. He looks into her eyes and sees himself flapping
in her like a fractured pigeon, red and brown
and shivering. The whited noise. The sudden altar

of a bus. The grace of violence under
wheel, under engine, underneath.

## Light as Imagined through a Body of Ice

An expansion into light, or we could have been, or were
for a moment. A painting is one kind of marriage

between permanency and sight, but another is the flame
of a photograph. Not our bodies themselves, itself,

but the brief kiss of radiation, too tired
in the morning to share with you its plans, a regular flash

of sheets against wall. You go to museums to fall in love
with the most impassioned strokes, to share the genuflections

of love. And then you go home to what works every day,
catch your glint of everything off the edge of the fork.

## String Theory

Take this drowning sea, where I am breathing
so deeply, blue rivulets—I mean the steam

of your being, up and up—
our memory, a child

into the mouth of the sky-
lights—and I'm as gone and happy with you
as the gray diadem of a clam, if clams could feel

doubt. I'm saying love
becomes the wish of coins blueing in the fountain.

We can aspire to be that small
carousel of metal that spins on the moment,

      and on nights like this it is okay
not to know but to feel, despite your being gone,
the chance happening. As it happens

      I know the difference between imagination and memory no more than this,

than you, but to live sometimes I dream
instead of speaking to your God. Don't give up, you said,

on me. It was a dolphin becoming
the water, a mustard seed. One definition
of faith is that which cracks granite, restraint. A memory:

remember another ocean where we—another we, or an actually—
are neither of us

dripping, on each other, our lips, our listening, our life

and jackets and the dance of the glistening city—granite
on the water, Cincinnati under one made-up face

we share in the moment. The light is candlelight, you're reading

I'm reading
                        your face
my face.

            If not exactly like this, at least in the sense that a fable makes
a living place. I'm saying I have considered, as we've all considered,

not being: we sat in hospitals for each other,
facing each of our fathers
trying not to leave: I am thinking of you tonight

and how once you consider death, really consider it, you realize
here we are, and what you've been considering is love.

# Heliocentric

*If I beg and pray you to set me free, then bind me more tightly still.*
Homer


I'm striving to be a better astronaut,
but consider where I'm coming from,

the exosphere,
a desk where the bluest air

thins to a lip. Impossible
to know the difference

from where I sit and space.
I promise

I still dream

of coming back to you—settling
on your yellow for the kitchen.

And we won't fight.

Not in this manifest. Not over the crumpled bodies
of laundry. We won't row
over the nail polish, its color,

the spilled sun. Inspiration
is the deadliest radiation.
It never completely leaves the bones.

You know.
From here,

there are no obstructions
but the radiant nothingness. An aurora

borealis opens

like a fish. This. To the pyramids, yes,
to a great wall. And there you are,

moving from curtain to curtain. O, to fantasize
of having chosen
some design with you.

But the moons over Jupiter. But
asteroids like gods
deadened by the weight of waiting. I remember

you said pastel

for the cabinet where the spice
rack lives. That I ought've picked you

up flowers when I had a chance. Daisy, iris, sun.
Red roses. Ultraviolet,
the color of love
(what else but this startles the air open

like an egg?).
I'm really trying

to be better, to commit
to memory the old songs about the ground,
to better sense your latitudes,

see the corona of your face.
Take your light

as it arrives. Earth is heavenly
too. But know that time is precious
here. How wine waits years and years to peak.

What is there to do: I've made love
to satellites in your name.

I'm saying I don't know
when I'll return. Remember me, for here are

dragons and the primitive song of sirens.
Stars that sway
elysian. Ships that will not moor, lovers

who are filled with blood and nothing
further. Who could love you
like this? Who else will sew you in the stars?

Who better knows your gravity and goes
otherwise, to catastrophe?

I've schemed and promised
to bring you back a ring

from Saturn. But a week passes, or doesn't

manage. Everything steers impossible
against the boundless curb of light.

Believe I tried
for you. Against space. Time

takes almost everything
away. To you. For you.
A toast to everything incredible. I almost wish

I'd never seen the sky
when always there was you. Sincerely,

# ABOUT THE AUTHOR

Keith S. Wilson is an Affrilachian Poet, Cave Canem fellow, and graduate of the Callaloo Creative Writing Workshop. He serves as Assistant Poetry Editor at *Four Way Review* and Digital Media Editor and Web Consultant at *Obsidian*. Keith works as an instructor and game designer in Chicago.

Poetry is vital to language and living. Since 1972, Copper Canyon Press has published extraordinary poetry from around the world to engage the imaginations and intellects of readers, writers, booksellers, librarians, teachers, students, and donors.

**WE ARE GRATEFUL FOR THE MAJOR SUPPORT PROVIDED BY:**

THE PAUL G. ALLEN
FAMILY FOUNDATION

TO LEARN MORE ABOUT UNDERWRITING
COPPER CANYON PRESS TITLES,
PLEASE CALL 360-385-4925 EXT. 103

WE ARE GRATEFUL FOR THE MAJOR SUPPORT PROVIDED BY:

Anonymous (3)

Jill Baker and Jeffrey Bishop

Anne and Geoffrey Barker

Donna and Matt Bellew

John Branch

Diana Broze

The Beatrice R. and Joseph A.
Coleman Foundation, Inc.

Laurie and Oskar Eustis

Mimi Gardner Gates

Nancy Gifford

Gull Industries, Inc. on behalf of
William True

The Trust of Warren A. Gummow

Petunia Charitable Fund and
advisor Elizabeth Hebert

Bruce Kahn

Phil Kovacevich and Eric Wechsler

Lakeside Industries, Inc. on behalf
of Jeanne Marie Lee

Maureen Lee and Mark Busto

Rhoady Lee and Alan Gartenhaus

Peter Lewis

Ellie Mathews and Carl Youngmann
as The North Press

Hank Meijer

Gregg Orr

Gay Phinny

Suzie Rapp and Mark Hamilton

Emily and Dan Raymond

Jill and Bill Ruckelshaus

Kim and Jeff Seely

Richard Swank

Dan Waggoner

Barbara and Charles Wright

Caleb Young as C. Young Creative

The dedicated interns and
faithful volunteers of
Copper Canyon Press

The Chinese character for poetry is made up of two parts:
"word" and "temple." It also serves as pressmark for
Copper Canyon Press.

.

The poems are set in Requiem.
Book design and composition by Phil Kovacevich.